01/24

INDIANA NOBLE SAD MAN
OF THE YEAR

POEMS BY STEVE HENN

INDIANA NOBLE SAD MAN
OF THE YEAR

POEMS BY STEVE HENN

Wolfson Press

Illustrations by Frannie, Lucy, Oren, and Zaya Henn
Design by Sky Santiago

ISBN: 978-1-939674-07-4

Wolfson Press
Master of Liberal Studies Program
Indiana University South Bend
1700 Mishawaka Avenue
South Bend, Indiana 46634-7111

FOR MY KIDS
ZAYA
FRANNIE
LUCY
OREN
THANK GOD I HAVE THEM

ACKNOWLEDGMENTS

"REQUIEM" FIRST APPEARED IN THE SUMMER '15 ISSUE OF *MIDWESTERN GOTHIC*

"POEM FOR THE GIRL NEXT DOOR" APPEARED IN THE WINTER '15/'16 ISSUE OF *THE CHIRON REVIEW*

"I'M PLEASED THAT MY BOY DANCES" APPEARED IN THE WINTER '15/'16 ISSUE OF *NERVE COWBOY*

"THIS ONE TIME" AND "THE LOTTERY WINNER" TO APPEAR IN THE SUMMER '16 ISSUE OF *THE CHIRON REVIEW*

"LOOKING FOR MY FATHER" APPEARED IN THE SUMMER '16 ISSUE OF *MISFIT MAGAZINE* (ONLINE)

"ALWAYS WANTED A CAREER IN EDUCATION? CLICK HERE" TO APPEAR IN THE FALL '16 ISSUE OF *RATTLE*

"MAKING SENSE OF THIS ELECTION" WAS SELECTED AS A *RATTLE* "POETS RESPOND" WINNER, APPEARING THE FIRST WEEK OF OCTOBER '16

CONTENTS

Foreword	11
The Dawning	21
39 and Counting	22
A Solid Idea	23
What Facebook Knows	25
Hey Internet!	27
Ode to Facebook	28
Making Sense of This Election	29
I'm Pleased That My Boy Dances	32
Father's Day, Fishing	33
Looking for My Father	34
Prosperity Gospel Made Easy	35
Today in 7th Period	36
Always Wanted a Career in Education? Click Here	38
Chasing the Dragon	39
A Friend of Nature	40
I Used to Smoke Pot	42
Perfectly Natural	44
Poem for the Girl Next Door	45
I Pity the Fool	48
Christmas Bonus	49
I Was a First Grade Creeper	51
The Mother Teresa Award for Transcendent Empathy and Exemplary Human Kindness	53
This One Time	55
The Lesson	56
My Fellow Americans DO NOT	58
Poetic Justice	59
Poem Written after Some Random Guy with a Clipboard at My Door Asks "Do You Have a Security System?"	60
A Crazy Little Thing	61
Requiem	62
A Hike around Town	63
Maturation	64
Motivational	65
Over the Top	66

Resolutions   68
The Lottery Winner   69
Growing Up in the Right Community   70
How It Could've Went Down in the Faculty Lounge   71
Frannie Launches My Modelling Career   72
Welcome to Dadland!   73
Single Dad Blues   74
Gratification   75
New Inscription at Ellis Island   77
Theories   78
Press Release, Moon Edition   80
Dear Internet,   81
Backyard Haiku   82
Sitting in a Plastic Lawnchair in
    My Own Backyard, Indiana, May 2015   84
Finale   86
Notes on the Poems   89
Notes on the Art   91
Gratitude   95

FOREWORD

Indiana Noble Sad Man of the Year is Steve Henn's third book of poetry. As in his previous volumes, Henn does hand-to-hand combat with the absurdity of daily life, including our experiences with the pervasive media—Facebook, cell phones, Internet ads, movies, self-promotion, and dreams—that can lead us astray. Although these new poems are born of the same live performance energy that produced his first two books, the new work shifts registers. We encounter similarly disturbing elements of modern culture, but most are more subtly infused into story and character. When he writes, for example, that Facebook is a "cockeyed apparatus … foisted like an albatross upon us," Henn doesn't leave us with a general indictment of the culture. The albatross, borrowed from Coleridge's poem, symbolizes the speaker's own guilt, his "compulsive" participation in the "raw, despairing and angry" behavior of social media interaction. At the heart of the book is a question about the self, even as the poems also describe an objective world we recognize. If this is an autobiographical work, a confession, it is one that explores common contemporary sources of shame. The fact that the poet owns his shame helps his readers to admit their own participation. Even in moments of outward mockery, the barb turns inward. "Poetic Justice" is a poem about a surprise confrontation with a former student who has become a door-to-door salesperson, a fate that the speaker derides. But the mockery reveals itself as an "old anger swelling," and the speaker's laughter is "delirious." In this way, the poem mocks mockery, and the question about our responsibility for others seeps almost to the surface of the text.

Henn dedicates this book to his four children, whose drawings and paintings serve effectively as illustrations. (In notes at the end of the volume, Henn relates the origins of some of the art works.) He selects his poems for this volume with the knowledge that his children are (or will become) its readers. The book might earn a PG rating if poetry publications were voluntarily policed by, say, the Academy of American Poets. It tells a father's story in a form that a child may begin to comprehend, but it speaks even more powerfully to adults. Every confession, every raw dream, nudges us—not asking us to acknowledge our collusion, but inviting us to recognize and empathize. By holding nothing back in the way of motives and emotions, he reveals the common childishness of adults in triumph as well as in defeat.

The book's title is, in effect, a short poem about the book. Its initial taut string of adjectives not only anticipates the language of many of the poems, but also foreshadows the dramatic tension that operates throughout the collection. Steve Henn's "Man of the Year" isn't the usual hero or successful person whose face appears on the cover of *Time*. He's the *sad* Man of the Year, a man whose sadness is award-winning in its depth and staying power. He's recognized for his exemplary loser status. If his sadness somehow raises him up, ennobling him, any sense of conventional nobility is undermined by that sadness, as well as by the adjectival use of "Indiana," not an iconic, beloved, or celebrated state. Maybe his courageous acceptance of his sad Hoosier existence ennobles him. Or is it inescapably sad to be someone of noble spirit in Indiana, forever lost to fame? It's noble to be sad, and it's sad to be noble here. It's also ordinary: the Indiana Sad Man of the Year is an Everyman. We're all recipients of this unheralded and unsought award, and we can only hope to nobly bear the knowledge of it in recognition that the award, this Midwestern badge of honor, bestows no recognition. We know who we are. In this respect, Henn's book is ambiguous—self-questioning, wandering, but also morally grounded in humility. From this solid, humble foundation, the poet sometimes launches fireworks.

Henn's poetry enacts a style of learning. In "Fathers' Day," we observe the speaker paying attention to his son's words and gestures and being transformed by the boy's perspective. Attention to others offers a respite from our private torments. A similar process occurs in "Poem for the Girl Next Door," where the experience of meeting up again with an acquaintance from his youth leads the speaker to confess that his life has failed to fulfill the happy fantasies taken from movies and fairy tales. Her life parallels his own. Henn explores and demonstrates the subtlety with which the fantasy-ridden adult wavers between truth and wishfulness in an attempt to evade the hardest questions. The stark honesty of the poem, an honesty about the path our thoughts take, reveals how regrets frame our memories, preserving the past at the expense of learning, so that we're never able to move forward. The poem is about the impossible struggle to believe again. Henn helps us to imagine the freedom that the speaker hasn't yet achieved.

The freshness of Henn's observations creates the sense that the insights are happening spontaneously, in the act of writing. *Tour de force* rants like "Motivational" and "Poetic Justice" also depend on Henn's superb ability to reproduce the actions of the mind. Each poem builds dramatically from a dreaded setup (a motivational speaker at school; a solicitor at the door) to the gleeful seizing of an opportunity for mockery—but in a manner that exposes the speaker's own faults, too. The irony isn't reflexive, but intrinsic to the character and situation of the speaker. No one escapes Henn's fine-tuned sense of justice, the force at the heart of the book. Henn's poems are at once critical and confessional, often using dramatic irony to turn the critical spotlight on the speaker. Still, he resists the compulsion to blame. Insofar as the poems are autobiographical, Henn shows compassion toward himself; the poems lead to laughter and release, and in this sense they are the expression of patience, with himself and with other people. Like Charles Bukowski or Alan Ginsberg, Henn broadens and deepens our feelings, opening the way to a humane existence in an absurd world.

The confessional mode unifies the book. The speaker—father, teacher, homebody, beer-drinker, music-lover, worrier, second-guesser, critic, dreamer—performs a complex, improvised routine. It's not stand-up so much as a one-man show of self-exposure. In each poem we have the sense of following a man in the act of discovering what he's about. A standout example is "Today in 7th Period," in which the teacher-speaker loses his way during an off-the-cuff pep talk to a classroom of kids who are suddenly paying attention only because they can't guess where his lecture is going. The poem gives us a dizzying insight into the experience of teachers, who often leap into an unplanned talk and find themselves in the nightmare position of wondering whether they can construct a sane finale to the mad sentence or expandable paragraph they've launched. The poem ends with a self-congratulatory "*Yesss.* Still got it." But we'll be the judge of that. Not every narrative here has a soft landing, but the splashdowns and crashes are artful and instructive. There is sometimes a flash of the miraculous, a healing word.

Henn's style is a further unifying element. Typically he produces a fast series of surprising adjectives or images, forcing us to adjust our expectations on the fly, to participate nimbly as interpreters, following closely like students of a schoolmaster who knows how to keep us on our toes. Sometimes the shifting of perspective is a method of layering and deepening, as in the funny passage two-thirds of the way through "The Mother Teresa Award," in which the poet imagines his former classmates coming home in the evenings from humiliating jobs, only to suffer through a maddening concatenation of degrading household disasters. In other instances, the strings of adjectives, images, or episodes work by way of irony, as in the pile-on of adjectives in the last line of "Over the Top," where the beautiful triumphant girlfriend is also the "ruthless" WWII Nazi of the speaker's grandfather's nightmares. The world of this book is one in which one person or one object can contain opposite forces and multitudes of meaning. In the end, it is difficult to blame the girlfriend when her innocent fun dredges up for the speaker the entire troubled history of his masculinity. In an ironically healthful way, the young woman, through her surprising arm wrestling victory, intervenes in the history of Western warfare. It is almost a blessing to be her victim.

Steve Henn's work participates in two current poetic trends, both of them tied to the broad "plain speech" movement coming out of the Romantic period in the poetry of William Wordsworth. The poetry slam circuit is one source of Henn's commitment to plain speech. A practiced performer of his own poems, he conceives of them almost as scripts, texts to be read aloud. Today's bardic tradition of oral poetry emphasizes personal expression. Its energy comes from the public stance that the poet takes as an individual personality, someone with a life story and a political mission. Such poetry is often confessional, dramatic, and argumentative—a poetry of voice rather than description. The other evident influence on Henn's language, attitude, and style is the tradition of working-class poetry as exemplified by Don Winter and Philip Levine, whom Edward Hirsch called "a large, ironic Whitman of the industrial heartland." That tradition is equally attached to the patterns of ordinary speech, but it strives for objectivity and the exploration of common experience, submerging its politics almost completely in narrative and descriptive details. Consider Don Winter's poem "Roofing" from his chapbook *On the Line* (MuscleHead Press, 2006):

> Mornings we ripped
> shingles. When air temp topped
> body temp we got buzzed.
> We sat and smoked.
>
> "I'd get monkeys
> to do your jobs
> if I could teach them not to shit
> on the roof," boss yelled.
>
> We laughed like struck
> match sticks. Down in the street
> sheets just hung there on the line
> like movie screens.

Although Henn's poetry is more flamboyant and personal, both poets are masters of economy, and neither balks at calling shit shit. It would be difficult to find a word to cut from the work of either. The language is already curtailed. Despite the bluntness of phrases like "we ripped/shingles" and "when air temp topped/body temp," there is something classical or formal about the movement of Winter's poem through the four-line stanzas: the full stops, the turn from workers to boss to workers, the placement of the boss's speech (the only spoken lines) at the center of the poem, and the muted revelatory conclusion. The two final figurative descriptions suggest both the passivity and the hidden power of the workers. The poem is a compact representation of lives in conflict. The boss's statement about monkeys suggests the structural violence of capitalism. The workers, typically enthralled by movie screens, light up with forced laughter, but united they seem capable of a greater conflagration.

Winter and Henn share the language of ordinary speech, but the discipline of Don Winter's political outlook is foreign to Steve Henn's poetry. We can see how his language differs from the style of Winter's in a passage from Henn's "Maturation," about the social life of the schoolyard:

> I was not privy to these Indian-style-seating
> roundpavement discussions with hands on knees,
> I was busy reluctantly exchanging coats
> with a frenemy who liked mine better than his
> and whose social circle I so wanted to penetrate

Here the speaker explains his first-grade alienation from the "mature" sixth-graders who sat talking during recess. This is psychological realism rather than materialism. Although the poet crafts precise images to describe circumstances and actions, the idiosyncratic phrasing is intended to represent the precise steps by which a particular mind processes experience. "Indian-style-seating/roundpavement discussions with hands on knees" is a memorable image partly because of the way it characterizes the speaker. The phrase "I was not privy" frames the statement as an adult observation, but the description of the seating arrangement calls back the childhood perspective in which the powwows of Hollywood Indians provide the only way of grasping the meaning of the discussion circle. Likewise, "frenemy" is a kid's concept, and it sinks the second independent clause into the social space of early grade school. The remembering adult organizes the long sentence into a logical, confessional explanation, but the child-self nevertheless survives there whole. To a Wordsworthian degree, Henn is faithful to this double perspective, demonstrating a keen adult responsibility toward the child within.

But philosophically, Henn is anti-Wordsworthian. He doesn't strive for transcendence. In his short poem "Sitting in a Plastic Chair in My Own Backyard, Indiana, May 2015" (a sort of parody of James Wright's famous poem, "Lying in a Hammock at William Duffy's Farm in Pine Island, Minnesota"), Henn seems purposely to set nature aside as irrelevant:

> A neighbor's mower just quit,
> bird sounds echo in the trees.
> The shriek of car and motorcycle
> to the distant right. Here, the maple tree. There
> the soccer net, the neighbor's still trampoline.
> I've got a novel, a book of poems,
> a notebook, and a lager.
> The kids are fed and settled.

The dishes stay undone.
I am not wasting my life.

Wright, like Wordsworth, turns to nature for inspiration, first reviewing a series of beautiful images ("the bronze butterfly," "the cowbells" that "follow one another/ Into the distances of the afternoon," the "sunlight between two pines," "the droppings of last year's horses" that "blaze up into golden stones"), then closing with a shockingly definitive statement, a realization: "I have wasted my life." In Wordsworth's Romanticism, nature is a spiritual reality, a living source of goodness and wisdom that can lift us out of our artificial social, commercial, and imaginative constraints. In Wright's poem the shock of the ending is really a way by which the speaker calls himself back to an awareness of the power of nature to inspire the imagination. The statement "I have wasted my life" is a spiritual recognition that shows promise of turning the page, escaping the busy world, and renewing connection to the source. For Henn, the natural world is present but mixed with and overwhelmed by man-made objects and human activities that cannot be transcended or escaped. Henn's poem ends with rewards, self-indulgent pleasures. The speaker turns to his beer and his books, having already dispatched his childcare duties. His final statement, rather than a definitive life assessment, sounds like a contingent judgment ("I am not wasting my life"—by doing the dishes, for example). The poem does not perform a gesture of purification. It leaves us in the messy, changeable realm of an ongoing, unpredictable life whose contingencies we can respond to but not master.

Wright's man in the hammock is an Everyman who has wasted his life by closing himself off from the spiritual resources of the natural world, and implicit in his final line is an accusation directed at the rest of us: "You have wasted your life." Henn's poem, however, offers no epiphany and also no definitive judgment. His poetry resists the temptation to funnel its observations into politics, philosophy, or religion. The "noble sad man" is bereft of such consolations. Is that a bad thing? Is it possible to say? Today, the news of the world rushes through us faster than our own lives, pulling us along, dragging us forward until we're out of breath, our attention torn into fragments. What can a poet do on a good day but sit in a plastic chair and read and write? As fantastical as *Indiana Noble Sad Man of the Year* is, it remains grounded in a humble, sad awareness of our fragmented post-religious, post-human world. Steve Henn will, I hope, continue to help us think about and imagine our fate in this world, a world that we'll move beyond only by moving through.

Joseph Chaney
Wolfson Press

But the thought of being a lunatic did not trouble him.
The horror was that he might also be wrong.
— George Orwell, from *1984*

THE DAWNING

Maybe it's the heat that's melted
something in my core otherwise jagged,
cynical or aloof here at Three Crowns Coffee

but when the first thing the homeless guy
alone on the couch says to me is "if you ever need
anything don't be afraid to ask," I don't laugh
or shake my head, I don't chuckle or guffaw
or break eye contact at this humanizing
and unprecedented offer of assistance
from a stranger even though it's curiously followed
by "nice to meet you" and "I'm here all the time"

which is not entirely true, seeing as he's not been
here any of the 10 or 15 times this summer
I've been in, drinking iced tea and jotting a few lines
or chatting up my 10-year-old daughter – still,

I'm struck and lifted, pleased and pacified and inspired
by such a gesture, so simple and dignified
from a man carrying clothes in plastic grocery bags,
a strip of rag run through his belt loops, knotted
and forming a tail there where the buckle would be
and I'm nearly embarrassed by his gracefulness

as he's leaving he says "be careful now, out in this heat"
sweet Jesus is this happening? Who is this man?
Do Saints exist? *Why do I feel like I'm going to cry?*
God in Heaven Who I'll wake up doubting tomorrow
or Something or Someone Up There or Out There tell me
this is what the world is coming to, I so much want
to believe in this, tell me this is where we start anew.

39 AND COUNTING

It takes a long time to lose
the feeling of being a young man.
Believe it or not, the penis
has nothing to do with it. Ha.
4 lines in and already I'm lying.
The sexual mind still goes
and goes at 39, that's true.
One feels generally less
like it's a personal psychosis
no one else experiences.
How many men do you know
who can still get it up
for whom mating is not tantamount?
None? One resists
feeling old. One is told
you're only as old as you feel.
Lies. Geologically speaking,
We're all dead already,
pebbles deposited carelessly
by the glaciers of space-time.
Earth time. Time immemorial,
a myth. It's not just
that you'll go, that I'll go,
that everyone we've ever known
or heard of will expire.
The whole damn species is bound
to go extinct. How foolish, those
who hold fast to the notion
we are on this planet to prevail.

A SOLID IDEA

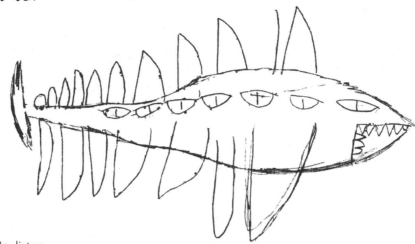

No, listen
what if people constantly carried around
    a buncha weird stuff in their stomachs   like sharks do
          like, what if the whole famdamnly is sitting around
    on the back deck burnin' weenies and lamenting
  the coming end of summer and Grandpa horks up a toaster oven
just coughs and gags and there it goes
      clangin' on the wood like the fallen fruit
of some strange mechanical tree and Grandpa, embarrassed
      wipes his mouth and grumbles   Don't remember eatin' that
and then what if Gramps chokes up a toilet plunger and Uncle Walt goes
    Seen that in the basement t'other day   Grandpa's in distress
and before you know it he's clutching his chest
        and falling over in the aluminum lawnchair gasping
    like a shark outta water   and Dad just stands there
with the weiner-flipper in his hand and goes
      Welp. Autopsy time!   and has at his father-in-law's
  midsection with various instruments of grilling and torture
mom's horrified   You're not gonna cook him! she gasps
      and sobs into her plastic disposable plate with the chips on it
and the pile of ketchup   and Dad goes Come on no, Nancy!
    Dammit! *Autopsy Time*!   and he swipes clean through
Grandpa's stomach and out spills a deck of nudie cards
  a bent discolored Wander Indiana license plate
    the shin bones of various medium-sized domesticated animals
random marbles   a Panama hat with a rip in the band
  a jar fulla baby teeth   and so on and so forth   and Dad goes
It's the motherlode, Nancy! We're puttin' this treasure pile on Ebay!
    and *people bid on it*   it's ridiculous   like nobody's ever SEEN
a jar of baby teeth from a 67-year-old white male's stomach for sale

so everybody wants one   one thousand, ten thousand
            one hundred thousand dollars!   and pretty soon you don't have to start out
        at community college cuz Dad can make a large enough
    donation to someplace lesser in the Ivy League   Brown, maybe
            and that is your ticket outta this town, brother
                                            whoooooooooooooooooosh
        hobknobbing with high society and datin' debutantes
    or whatever the heck they've got up there
            wouldn't that be great? Man, *dang*
        . . . how can we make that happen?

WHAT FACEBOOK KNOWS

An algorithm on FB predicts I'm a single
dad and markets some cheesy T-shirt to me
about my giant heart, presumably so worthy
of the adulation of others that I ought to say so
on my beer belly everywhere I go, a convenient advertisement
probably intended to attract single moms to the hearth
like bugs to my neighbor's blue zapper –zzzzt!
I doubt they have a similar shirt for moms,
right? There's no, I have a vagina, I raise my kids
solo, somebody give me a f**kin' Academy Award t-shirt
– Big T-Shirt must be too busy fighting breast cancer
by sexually objectifying the unfortunate boobs of the victims
to get into the whole gender-equality angle.
I may, however, be just morally suspect enough
to buy the damn thing, in green, cuz my ancestors
were Irish, you know, and everybody needs a goddamn
stereotype to fulfill, and then wear it to Walmart
and to the public playground and try to look regal
and noble and too good to accept your pity but
perfectly willing to accept your phone number, perfectly
willing to exploit a basic reality of my life for sexual advantage,
because that, don't let anyone tell you different,
is what being human is all about. Then another time FB
pegged me as a rage filled psychopath
with an arsenal in a fortified basement bunker
by trying to sell me a T-shirt the message of which
went something like "Gun Control is Stupid
because if you touch my daughter I will murder you,
you Commie Lib!" That's a minor approximation but definitely
true to the spirit of the exact wording. They were way off
on that one, although I've never observed a teenage boy
with no impulse control drooling over my oldest,
so you never know. The creepy one, though,
I just want to warn you this is going to be odd and awkward
for all of us, it's a strange thing, FB apparently knew
a strange detail about my life, they knew something
I'd not communicated to anyone, see, they tried to sell me
Sensodyne toothpaste for sensitive teeth, and it was true
that there'd been some blood lately, post-brushing,
well, regular blood, blood without flossing – who flosses?
You sick freaks. I hadn't TOLD anybody though.

That's the sort of the thing back in the day I might admit
to a Priest, but I'm certainly not posting it as a status update:
"Bless me Father for I have sinned, my mouth is bleeding,
it's like my own personal corporeal Biblical plague, WTF
have I done to so wickedly upset Thee?" But FB knew,
they knew my gums were bleeding, so maybe they actually
knew I would kill someone who laid a harmful
and/or sexual hand on my daughter, so maybe
they're right that I'll exploit what people tend to see
as a more tragic circumstance than single motherhood –
that is, single fatherhood – on my way to being named
Indiana Noble Sad Man of the Year 2015, I prefer
the award be made of bronze, I'd like to ask
the ghost of Kurt Vonnegut to introduce me.

HEY INTERNET!

Do you know any single ladies
looking for a man no games
because I haven't heard about any
for the last 20 minutes of my personalized
Facebook advertising   I have to admit
"no games" disappoints   A first date
without a 3-hour round of Monopoly
is a pretty sorry experience IMHO
If the economic domination of
a fanciful Atlantic City doesn't put the zest
in her goosestep then perhaps Risk
random chance and military strategizing
being two great tastes that taste great together
like my chocolate in her peanut butter
My friend Joe says I'd like to see a
(challenging) boardgame called Monogamy
and I'm a pretty witty guy too, I can zing
like a king, so to continue the thread I said
Hey Joe, that sounds like the most
challenging game of all! Joe clicked "like"
but I bet it was closer to a ROFL, IMHO.

ODE TO FACEBOOK

"O cruel, needless misunderstanding! O stubborn, self-willed exile from the loving breast!"
> — George Orwell, from *1984*

O Cesspool of Reactionary Politicizing!
O Vast Virtual Kingdom of the Ill-Advised Overshare!
O Repository of Unnecessary Relationship Details!
O Strange and Not Altogether Wonderful Catalogue of the Collective Id!

hear me now and believe me later
Wherefore shall I extricate the baubles of my attention from your unlikely snares?
How, exactly, can you be so unwholesomely compulsive?
Why, however, do I behave in your ever-present forum
    in ways raw, despairing and angry I would not otherwise express
    with so little taste and/or discretion?

Zuckerberg, O Zuckerberg, You Magnificent Bastard,
                        You Dev'lish Tempter of 1/7th of the Mortal Souls of Earth,
what cockeyed apparatus have you wrought and foisted like an albatross upon us?

MAKING SENSE OF THIS ELECTION

Last night I dreamt I was running for Vice President
against Donald Trump and Mike Pence on the
Higgins/Henn/Mevis ticket. Ben Higgins is the guy from here
who became TV's *The Bachelor* and has such a sparkling charm
and wit to him that *Saturday Night Live* spoofed him in a sketch
called "The Bland Man." I learned this from my daughter. I don't watch
Saturday Night Live – I pass out on the couch Saturdays around the time
it airs, after Notre Dame football finally ends. Andrew Mevis
is this kid in my AP English class who is a nationally ranked
high school football punter. Apparently it took
two of us to fill out the VP portion of the ticket. Actually it was sort of
like running for President of Warsaw, Indiana, because we were in
this big public building like the Center Lake Pavilion with
metal folding chairs set up in rows and a microphone on a stand
and a screen and projector and we were going to do presentations.
Trump presents, we present – rather than debate. Like we're being called
in to talk to the community like one of those shysters in the Education
field who quit teaching to travel around and tell working teachers
what their attitude should be about teaching and generally how
they might avoid failing children miserably for the rest of their lives.
So Trump blah blahs a lot, makes a lot of promises, the usual, and Ben
and Andrew and I are standing at the back of the big room
scheming, plotting how to upstage the Orange One and Ben
goes, I got this, don't worry about it, you don't have to say
anything, I'm gonna nail this, just back me up. But when
we get up to the mic, me and Mevis standing behind Ben
with our arms folded like a couple-a wannabe hardasses,
(Mevis can pull it off, he's large and muscular, I am not,
I am large and not muscular, I fake it). what actually happens
is Higgins steps up to the mic and the Bland Man has nothing
to say. He opens his mouth and a great void of nothingness
spills out, a giant empty space, like his whole speech
was written by a nihilistic existentialist who doesn't believe
in having things to say, so I have to cover for him – we can't
embarrass ourselves, we have to say something, and I rant and rave
about various things political, I honestly don't remember, I think in my
dream state I had an impression of myself as being a powerful truth teller,
but I'm sure if my psyche or God or someone could transcribe
the monologue to show me while awake it wouldn't've made
any sense. I often have the sensation of making sense while
on some more elemental level I know I'm not making sense

in my dreams. So I sit down on the small rising of the stage
after speaking and Trump is furious – I've called him out,
I've exposed him somehow, or tried to, and he marches to me
and threatens to hit me and I'm like "hit me" and I sit there
sullen with my shoulders sloped like I'm about to take some
asinine punishment that deep in my marrow I feel I've earned
from my Catholic forebears or my Hoosier neighbors or the
more virtuous poets or some such, but Trump throws these haymakers
all around me, left and right, up and down, past my head,
behind my back, and he never hits me, he's too chickenshit
to make good on his threat but he has to make a big show of
appearing to be a tough guy, and . . .
maybe that was the point of the dream, you know?
Maybe I wanted to tell myself something about Trump
that was already patently obvious to all of us, I mean,
that could've been it, that could've been why my head
went through all of that. Jesus. What a waste.

I'M PLEASED THAT MY BOY DANCES

I know, that sounds like the title
of a David Bowie song, but it's not,
it's a commentary on my five year old son's
capacity for boogie. When I was 5,
my older siblings used to put *Disco Duck*
or *Steve Miller Band Greatest '74-'78*
on the turntable (turntables weren't hip then,
they were the only technology available
that wasn't 8-track tapes) and I'd stand
there like I was holding a guitar
and I'd shake a leg. One leg. Repetitively.
And I'd want to bust a move
but also felt self-conscious, my brothers
and sister wanting a show and me never
even hollering "gimme a beat!" or asking
to be called Mr. Henn Esq. "if you're nasty."
But when my boy hears *Jungle Love*
and it's driving him mad, making him crazy, crazy,
he contorts, twists, flips, bounces, boogies –
just like the floor exercises in the Olympics!
He puts all of himself into feeling
the groove. He's not embarrassed. He demands
acknowledgment for kinesthetically losing his mind.
Good for him! Good for my son,
and the undiminished grin on his face.
Good for his whole, new, unbroken,
and very wiggly bones.

FATHER'S DAY, FISHING

Did you see that Dad? my boy
said from the grass behind the seawall
that's quite a cast
for a five year old he said
I wish I were so
unconsciously witty
later he said I almost
got it in that boat
I said that would not
be good he said let's go
there and gestured
like Caesar Augustus at the public
pier presently I worried
he'd fall in then his lure
stuck in the rope in the water
that anyone can swim under
if they want to go beyond
but no one does because
social norms I dropped to a knee
set my rod down reached
into the water and while prying
his lure from the rope I wasn't
thinking quite as much about dying

LOOKING FOR MY FATHER

after John Berbrich

I see you in the likeliest faces.
A gray man piloting a family-filled car,
small like your Fiat, but not purple.
A tall man in the checkout line –
it's something in the eyes – the weariness,
the yearning. At home, in my own way
of silly joking coinflipped
with moody snark when the kids annoy.
In my mechanical ineptitude. In thinking,
thinking, *I'm under a lot of pressure boys,*
I s'pose your mother wants me to eat, always
thinking, thinking. Were I adopted,
I'd still be your son. I've never come home
with a new car bought at sticker price
in manic glee, but I have gone weeks
barely sleeping, giving away all my books
and music to strangers. That's half a life ago,
when I lost your navy jacket on the steps
of a closed Catholic church wandering Ithaca
at 3 a.m. I still have the camel's hair blazer,
one elbow worn through. It doesn't fit
anymore. Sometimes when I pester the kids
I hear your wife's voice, not yours, escaping
my throat. Sometimes I dream you stayed alive
and left and were angry at me
when I went looking for you.
I can be in my head, or singing in the car,
or looking sharply at the kids in the rearview
as you did with us, looking for you, looking,
and you're nowhere to be found.

PROSPERITY GOSPEL MADE EASY

It's simple. Jesus wants you to be rich!
Rich! Really, really rich! Try saying so
without smiling: My Lord and Savior
Wishes to Bless Me with Fruits of Abundance!
To multiply your bounty, make sure a minimum
of ten percent ends up in the collection plate!
We've got to keep the lights on at the megachurch,
the cappuccino frothing in our on-site coffee bar,
to be sure we're giving God His just desserts.
Own stocks! Own bonds! Buy Northrop Grumman!
Buy Halliburton! Buy assault rifles!
Finance the efforts of our Soldiers for Christ!
The message of the Christ is for your Faith
you ought to be awash in greenbacks! Doused in dollars!
Keep the party goin' through the thousand years of peace, son!
Feed the poor? Nah. Heal the sick? Not so much . . . it's true
Jesus said the likelihood of a rich man entering Heaven
is the same as a camel passing through the eye
of a needle, but in the O.G. Original Greek he then
produces a needle with a camel-sized hole in it!
I'll be damned! Or rather, not really!
Glory be, glory be, all things are possible,
especially the things you like!
Jesus definitely wants you to be filthy, stinking, dirty,
creepy, crawly, worldly, holy-rolly superior-soulely,
rrrrrrrrrrrrrrrrrrrrrrrrrich!

TODAY IN 7ᵀᴴ PERIOD

We were in the computer lab and the kids
were talking and laughing, having fun
which means they weren't getting *educated*
which ought to be an awful experience
via heavy reading and heavier silence,
perhaps pierced by a heavy sigh
which exhaled solidifies and clunks on the carpet
like a fat brick of wanting only to die
but instead they laughed and carried on, so I shouted
in my middle-aged cracking voice "perHAPS
you should be working on your ReSEARCH for your BibBIES
rather than" and here normally I'd say *talking about
your hot date this weekend with Johnnie Sue* – but
instead I ad-libbed, saying "rather than conversing as if . . .
sitting at a . . . coffeehouse . . . discussing . . . *boys*
and . . . politics . . ." and everybody looks over at me
on my orange plastic chair in the corner by the printer
like *what the hell kind of comment is that, Mr. Henn?
Are you ok? I mean are you having a breakdown?*
I didn't know what to do, so I continued, "and your friend
is wearing a scarf you find hideous so you compliment it
with baldfaced . . . facetiousness . . .

and you haven't seen a squirrel in 4 MONTHS
you're wondering if the laundry is done at home
because . . . you want to . . . treat yourself to . . .
clean pants tomorrow. . ." I heard snickers, I'm losing them,
what had started as an attempt at witty improv
had grown strange, weird and oddly gregarious
like a 45-pound tumor removed from Grandma's stomach
that grew a mouth and legs and started selling
vacuum cleaners door to door *so I kept going*
"and your friend keeps referring to her mom
as *mother* which she's never done before, as in
mother wants me home at eight or mother says
not to tell about what is in the man-sized freezer
in the cellar, and you're thinking *what's with this*
mother business? and then the golden boy you love
in secret from a distance by burning incense
in your bedroom and clumsily consulting tarot cards
haphazardly, without conviction but in desperation
walks into the coffeehouse and orders that weird tea
they make by steeping tiny twigs and you jump,
you wail and say *No! You can't be serious!*
You're more alluring than all that! and he looks at you
just like, *oh, I guess you exist, but that doesn't interest me*
and there go all your imagined schemes to pull off
the perfect prom!"

You could hear the proverbial pin drop.
Not a word was uttered for the rest of class.
Yessss. Still got it.

ALWAYS WANTED A CAREER IN EDUCATION? CLICK HERE

I went into teaching, obviously,
to create a vast network of lackeys
reaching beyond their decades
of graduation to infiltrate communities
with my nefarious values. And to create
yes-men. Yes-people. Yes-women, too.
LBGTQ yes-folk. Equal opportunity yessing.
Everyone can agree with me.
Everyone can do what I say.
When their hands raise in class my lackeys know
the only appropriate comment is "tell me what
to think of this, Mr. Greatest Poet
in the Universe," and I say, Sally, Billy, whatever,
you're free to think exactly as I think
as much as you'd like. Sarah. Sam. Whoever
you are or may be – Christ, they stick me
with 120-150 of you whiners per semester,
you'd think God or Allah or the Hindi Elephant God,
whoever's in charge, ought to know
I've got more students in here than I can keep track of.
"Yes, Mr. The Greatest English Teacher in Known
and Unknown History," my students answer kindly,
gracefully, gratefully. "We understand you,
Mr. Don't Worry We Love You," they coo,
they soothe. "We were put here, in your presence,"
they confess, "so that you might be understood."
An otherworldly glint shimmers in their eyes
which I choose to ignore; it's like the palms
of their hands are pushing against my heels –
I go up and up and up, ever onward
into the light, understood, appreciated, elevated,
probing heaven with my hands
as if this were my coronation.

CHASING THE DRAGON

I like a classroom electric,
like we've incidentally plunged our pinkies
into a mild, not-too-painful,
intellectually edifying wall socket

Witticisms abound, I find myself
saying "that's a sharp comment"
frequently, as we dig into the frequencies
of what we've read, seen, heard

I like a classroom where the blood bubbles,
the brain sazzles, the lymph lubricates
inner pathways of circulatory knowledge,

where we're surprised when the bell rings,
where no one's thinking about the places they'd rather be.

A FRIEND OF NATURE

We've biked to the park,
my daughter and I, we're sitting
at a picnic table, she reads, I grade,
two ducks wander inquisitively over,
a woman duck, a duck man.
"We've got nothing for you" I say
in a voice strategically emptied
of malicious intent, tweaked and twinged,
or trying to be, with gentleness,
with small concern. I sit still.
I do not move suddenly. It reminds me,

I tell Lucy, of my old friend
who saw that body language is
the language of the animal kingdom,
that our posture and stance communicate
our intentions, that if we speak and mean
no harm, it is good to speak gently,
it may even be better to speak not at all.
Who's this friend, Lucy asks,
and I say, oh, he's not around anymore.

I don't tell her of the last story
to circulate about my old pal,
when he was down South in the renowned college town,
was beaten by a man at a party
and retaliated. The knife with which he spoke back
to his assailant, I do not mention. Where he is kept now,
unmentioned. "Once, we went fishing,

at the pond behind the Bob Evans,"
I tell her. A turtle crawled up
onto a half-submerged log. My friend
sat on a bucket, easy, made no sudden moves,
held his pole still, and whispered just a few words
to the creature, his posture speaking no harm,
his mouth repeating as if assuring an unfamiliar dog
or a scared child, "it's okay . . . it's okay
. . . I'm not going to hurt you."

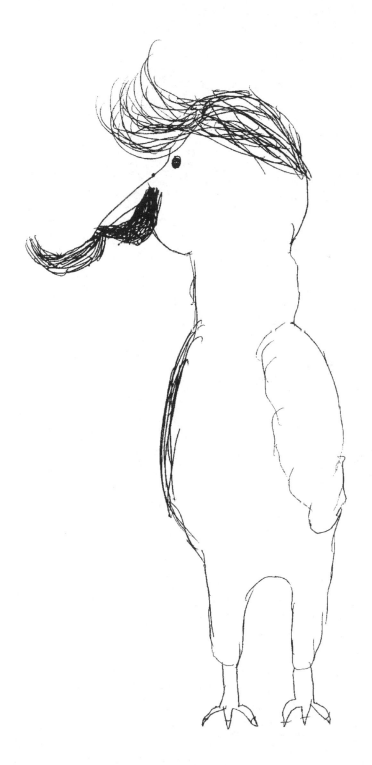

I USED TO SMOKE POT

for Dan

Nothing in Life makes you feel more
like a slathering, burping, drooling mammal
than an attack of the munchies.
That's why I don't smoke pot.
I am also not always gifted with
a finely-calibrated awareness of the social graces
and nuances necessary to avoid looking
and sounding like an assclown in public –
this is another reason I don't smoke pot.
I'm already clueless. On pot, it's like cluelessness
is powered up in my brain like I'm on
the 11th level of Suck in the video game called Real Life.
I'm bipolar too. I don't say this to commiserate
or to squeeze pity out of you. These days
I consider it a subtle sort of bipolar – it's refined,
with my medication and without the pot. It's classy.

It brings out poetry that pleases me. It's the kind
of bipolar Donald Trump wishes he was. But back-when,
not even while high, but even in rough temporal proximity
to some occasion of highness, my manias were
profoundly maniaier and my lows hit bottom
like a depth charge filled with lead pudding
sinking into a sea of shameless and self-aggrandizing
self-pity and despair. Also I would cry and freak out
and stress over imaginary things – I would think
people were following me! People *were* following me!
I REALLY MEAN IT. When I was high, PEOPLE
WERE FOLLOWING ME WITH BAD INTENTIONS.
I'm not presenting this as any sort of direct value judgment
on whether or not you, yourself, personally, in your private life,
should smoke pot. I'm here to equal-opportunity piss off
the Nancy Reagans and the Deadheads. But for me,
thinking well is a good thing. And it's hard enough when not high
for me to think well, which is why when I was young
and my girlfriend was pregnant and I was going back
to college for the second (or was it third?) time,
when my brother, younger than me, a college senior,
sat me down and put his hand on my shoulder like he was
the older one, and said, "don't get high. You're a better person
without it," I feel very fortunate that, rarely and thankfully,
I was of a mind to take what he said seriously.
I was sober, and thinking, and predisposed to listen.

PERFECTLY NATURAL

See that man
He's following me
The *organization* he represents
has rigged an elaborate ruse
to convince me he's not following me
Like he's already at the cookie shop when I arrive
But he's reading a thick book in a showy way
Like, nobody here but us book readers, just here
reading a book, me and you buddy, cookie shop book readers,
Come talk to me and I will infiltrate your subversive circle
of poets and musicians and art-supremacists
He's sitting right behind me He wants me to say something
I can hear him breathing hoooo-pahhhh, hoooo-pahhh,
mimicking Darth Vader because he knows I get the joke
I am not going to talk to him I will not talk to him
He gets up to toss trash, bumps into a "coworker" at the door
This "coworker" is also a part of this elaborate ruse of undercover surveillance
"Are you going in?" he says. She laughs "not til four!"
A ha ha ha. A ha. A hah. Titter titter. Two normal local "workers" sharing a joke
But this is no joke.
He obviously is trying to get me to say things to him
He obviously wants to know things about our plans
To replace hymnals with profane poetry in every church in the county on Easter Sunday
I don't tell him anything I will never tell him anything they can't make me talk
He is headed out of doors. He is headed across the street. A car honks
as he crosses and he waves casually, just a normal local book-reading
Darth Vader-imitating "worker" having a casual day waving to cars casually
That was very clever
I have to give them that
If I didn't know better I would think that was perfectly natural.

POEM FOR THE GIRL NEXT DOOR

Hey Jody,
we're old now aren't we? but you'll always be
my archetypal girl-next-door.
One time while I was still married
and I saw you out in front of your dad's house,
you said you used to see me put my face
to the glass of the kitchen window,
peer across the yard, into your house,
trying to catch a glimpse of you.
You always knew I adored you,
didn't you? I used to live for
sneaking peeks of you sunbathing in a folding lawn chair
down in the grass below your screened-in porch.
Hey Jody, I wanna tell you something,
and I want you to feel the truth of it: you're still beautiful.
It's true we've aged, both of us –
I never thought I'd have a gut like this,
never knew I'd have this beer habit
to quench my anxiety.
I've had some hard times. So've you.
I can see it in your worn out eyes,
I can hear the hesitation in your voice,
like you're asking the world not to hurt you anymore.
I've heard this-and-that about what you've been through
and I s'pose maybe you've heard this-and-that
about me. I heard you lost your head for awhile.
I heard you didn't get custody of your children.
I don't know details, really. I just know
you've had your share of suffering, of pain.
Jody, did you know for two horrific stretches
of '96 and '99 I convalesced unwillingly
in Bloomington Hospital's psych ward?
Listen, when we talked just now
at the neighborhood barbecue, it felt like
the opening scene of a chick flick, just for a moment,
like act one of a movie – I know it's probably bullshit,
I'm not asking you to really take it seriously,
I blame it on *Silver Linings Playbook*. But listen,
I just want you to know, just because I felt that way
and just because I'm writing this, it doesn't mean
I'm gonna turn into your personal creeper, ok?

I haven't written a poem worth a damn in months.
God bless you for making me feel like
I've got things to say again. But
life's not a movie, and neither fairy tales nor suspense thrillers
seem to happen for me anymore.
Do you remember what it was like to play basketball
on your dad's backyard court with Jamie and Jennifer
one time, in middle school?
That's one of the first times I ever remember flirting
with anyone. I still don't know how to do it.
My jokes are always inappropriate,
my casual discussions dripping with TMI.
Just now, at 37, I can do barely passable small talk.
I liked hearing that little bit about what you're going through.
In my experience people don't often say things that are honest and true.
You had a husband who expected you to straighten out,
read his Holy Book, have dinner on the table every night,
do the things he thinks a woman should. I had a wife who
lost her head, at one point we tried to get it together by going
to church, but I don't trust any holy book, I've never felt God
inside a sterile building. It's not like we didn't inflict our share
of pain on them, I s'pose we did, but Jesus, Jody,
we're pushing 40, sometimes doesn't it all just wear you down?
I worry that I can't keep this up, job, house,
parenting, paying bills, paying taxes, sleeping alone
in my house when the kids are gone, taking pills for 14 years now
to keep my head straight, to keep from crumbling fast
by crumbling slow. Do you remember, one time, you came to
our back porch carrying the latest *Beckett Monthly*
and some of your dad's baseball cards? I do.
I remember I didn't know how to flirt then either,
you were so cute when you giggled, it made my cheeks flush.
You didn't care too much about the pretext of the cards,
instructed by your dad to only trade equal values,
and me not knowing what to do or say but Andre Dawson this
and Pete Rose that and you just chatting and beaming,
glowing and smiling like you always used to do.
Hey Jody, you look so tired and beautiful,
you're like a character in a Bob Dylan song.
You're a sculpture of a goddess who made herself mortal
for a lover, you're happy lyrics accompanied on acoustic guitar
in a minor key. Hey Jody, I really mean it, you're as beautiful
as you ever were, but all my friends are older now,
you're older too, and isn't it sad we've come this far

and yet we have this look in our eyes that says
What do I do? What do I do?

I PITY THE FOOL

I wish Jesus would've been
a little more like Mr. T. Ok,
a lot more. With the mohawk
and the gold chains. It would've made
His answers to those "tell me, Rabbi" questions
in the New Testament both highly entertaining
and pleasingly formulaic, like a good *Saturday
Night Live* comedy sketch with a memorable
catchphrase. Tell me, Rabbi – can a rich man
enter heaven? *I Pity the Rich Fool Who Try
to Enter My Father's Kingdom!* Just like that.
No elaboration. Mr. T Jesus would not be known
for His elaboration. He gets to the point.
Tell me, teacher, if a Levite is beaten
on the highway, who should stop and help him?
I Pity the Jew Who Doesn't Stop and Help!
Not even a Bible verse for reference. Maybe
Mr. T Jesus would organize a game of kickball
among the local prostitutes and tax collectors,
everybody on one side lines up to kick in order
and He goes *I Pity the Fool Who Line Up First
He Shall Be Last* – and He yanks at the scrawny
tweaker with the track marks at the back and
moves her to the front of the line. I suppose
Christian Punk Bands would have a helluva good time
mimicking Mr. T Jesus style lohawk mohawks,
but the gold chains, I don't know . . . I guess
He'd hand them out in bunches, giving them
away to followers and instructing them to go forth
and multiply these riches, as the pre-A-Team-reboot Jesus
told so clearly in the story of the servants and the talents.

CHRISTMAS BONUS

Once, I worked in a factory
and I got a canned ham
for a Christmas bonus.
The card that came with read
"To supplement your minimum
wage with no benefits, here's
something to keep you from starving
on your week off, yours truly,
Scrooge McOwnership."
I couldn't complain though.
I was bad at the work.
My doohinkeys didn't do the hinky
rightly, a hilariously low level
of hinkiness, in fact, in what I did.
When they brought out the hams
I laughed out loud – I was 19,
I thought it was some campy joke,
but the mostly thirtysomething workers
glared at me like I'd just
euthanized their grandmothers.
One silent night they began shorting
my paycheck without firing me.
One holy night, I walked out,
loose change jingling in my pockets,
jingling all the way.

I WAS A FIRST GRADE CREEPER

At Sacred Heart Elementary in 1982
reading *Dick and Jane* books under
the gentle guidance of Sister Colleen,
I was a first grade creeper.
In the next row up one seat
bathed in a saintly glow I'd associate
in years to come moreso with *Playboy*
than with the Stations of the Cross, sat Stephanie –
she of the long straight full dark hair
the full cushiony red lips
and the bemused, embarrassed,
why-are-you-still-looking-at-me smile,
looking back over her soft right shoulder
blushing and grinning and asking with her eyes
no really, weirdo, why are you still looking
at me with that very odd smile?

Though creeper-like my love was pure,
was true, bespectacled in brown plastic frames
with plastic lenses, awkward, self-conscious,
the yearning hair of my love combed straight down
in thick brown hunks on my forehead,
my earnest love, my holy love
untouched by unclean thoughts of physical coupling
beyond the chaste lip-bonding or hand-holding
in my confused and terrified fantasies
too young to sully my thoughts with so-called filth,
feeling for her a holy love of wonder as she'd look back
at me in embarrassment and ask herself what's going on
with this tall skinny kid spending all this time
staring and staring and staring at me?

It was a magical time, but I got over it.
I'd matriculate to second grade where an older boy
told me what sex was in full icky detail
and I began having graphic dreams
involving Princess Leia in the metal bikini
(on my lap) but that's a different crush . . .

I saw her again in CCD, in Catechism class
I had to take before Mass in seventh grade because

the middle school was public. Stephanie explained
to someone loudly and with full false prevarication
that she left Catholic School after first grade
because they made her go to mass EVERY day
sit there with the hymns and the incense
and the creepy old guy in the green robes
EVERY day and God, she just couldn't stand it.

Who are these parents, I wondered,
who pull their kid from Catholic School
at a seven-year-old's request, and where,
I wondered, can I get some, and why,
I wondered, why are you lying Stephanie,
why do you have to tell lies about it –
because it's just not true they made us
go to Mass every day . . .

THE MOTHER TERESA AWARD FOR TRANSCENDENT EMPATHY AND EXEMPLARY HUMAN KINDNESS

Dear Sam,

I don't know why you need to call
50 or 60 people from our high school
graduating class and attempt long,
one-sided, overly intense monologues
and question-and-answer sessions
concerning Sam's High School Experience –
like the conversation we had 6 or 7 years ago,
where you asked all the questions
and you provided all the answers.
I can't say I understand this obsession, Sam,
this apparent notion that your life
has been permanently and irrevocably damaged
by your high school experience, it's really sad,
it seems really sad, it seems a really sad
and unhelpful and largely fruitless fixation
that probably provides not even the coldest comfort
in the empty righteous sense that you've been wronged,
but I do know, Sam, that it's not as simple as calling you
nuts and leaving it to hang there in the air
like your interminable voice, the voice of a frustrated
motivational speaker haranguing his subjects
in hopes of what? – inspiring a frenzy of apologies,
a colossal pile of earnest pleas for forgiveness
ending in a welcoming-into-the-fold, a long-sought nuzzling
in the arms of the cool kids right there at the swell
of the warm and loving breast of popularity?
That is not the world, Sam. That is not what happens
in the world, Sam, and I can't believe you've gone this far
in life without knowing it, and I know, too,
another thing you should know: It's fucking rude, dude.
It's incredibly rude. The calling of people's parents,
the tracking down of work or home or cell numbers,
the self-centered plea for understanding – people
have jobs and spouses and children, people have their own
problems, Mike or Bill or Jerry or Jeff or somebody else
you've tracked down at 5:30 p.m. just got home from
an ass-chewing by a do-nothing manager at work,

they just fought over who does the dishes with the wife,
their kid just pooped on the floor, their dog just ate it,
the dog's about to puke it up, their spouse has a weak stomach
and can't clean it up without gagging so it's up to them –
in short, people have their own shit-shows to deal with,
Sammy, and they do not exist on this earth as your
former classmate to solve your hangups. I'm sorry,
but I mean *damn*. I know this is no kind of poem
that will win me the Mother Teresa Award
for Transcendent Empathy and Exemplary Human Kindness,
it's no kind of poem that will be praised for its poise
and wisdom, but you're not a child, and you should know, dude,
you should know what effect you're having on people.
You should maybe shut up, and maybe listen long enough
for somebody to tell you.

THIS ONE TIME

The liquor store clerk challenged me
to spell "diarrhea": d – i – a – r – r – h – e – a!
Boom! The repeat elementary school spelling bee champion
rides again! *I should get my beer for free*, I'm thinking,
and on the drive home, *the world should work this way.*
If I'm pulled over for the 62 I'm doing in this 45:
Sir, are you aware of how fast you were going?
Are you talking about speed, officer? V – e – l – o – c – i – t – y?
Very well then, Mr. Henn. You can spell. Go about your business.
Talk about these-aren't-the-droids-you're-looking-for!
Wouldn't that be great? Rather than tiering flight boarding
according to who paid for premium tickets, for example,
people would board by spelling acumen. National Spelling Bee
Champions now boarding. Next, National Finalists. National
Finalists, now boarding. Next, Regional Champions.
I'd be on with regional qualifiers which would have to give me
an advantage over like 98% of the population!
What comes next is equal opportunity where all can transcend poverty
with proper syntax and pronunciation. Secret, though,
secret secret, I've got a secret: in both 5th and 6th grade
at the Regional I didn't do so well. Out on the first word
both times. One of the words I've repressed from memory
because to recall would be too painful and the other was
"balloon." That tricky double-L. The Champ, though?
His story's even sadder. He went from a childhood reading entire editions
of the Encyclopedia Britannica to calling up and harassing
old classmates, fixating on how he was treated and by whom.
There are restraining orders, and he's not allowed near
the local high school. I'm not even saying this to be funny.
It's true. Any of my old Sacred Heart Elementary classmates
could look at him, a Lincoln Lion, and point at me, a local Viking,
and say, you're lucky, Steve. You're very blessed. That could've been you.

THE LESSON

for KTH

Once when young, I rode
my black generic BMX bike
along the bright-lit sidewalk
on a midsummer day. At the place
where the pavement ends,
supplanted by a dip into a yard-sized
field of lawngrass, a bird shit on me
and immediately the front wheel
detached from the bike. I tumbled,
scraped, fell. Left arm and mop of hair
beshitted, I had to ring the front door bell
at home – the door was locked.
When my sister answered I told her
what had happened and she laughed,
she laughed and laughed. Nothing
ever happens for a reason.

MY FELLOW AMERICANS! DO NOT

knock on my door in all manner of weather
but most especially in June, most especially on sunny days,
and offer to perform services in exchange
for the contents of my wallet. I don't want
my driveway seal-coated. I like my outdated
energy inefficient front window *just the way it is*,
the same way my mom used to love me
when I was six. I am not impressed
that you just unscrewed the head of a spray bottle
and licked the all natural toxin-free cleaning solution
from the dangling plastic straw. Ew. What's wrong with you?
Are you ok? Never mind. Don't answer that. I don't care.

I would rather invite you to the backyard
to knock back Stroh's after Stroh's and hear all about
the religion of your politics or the politics of your religion
than proffer currency in exchange for dubious handiwork
that is nonetheless better than I can do but never you mind
because I won't be doing it myself either. Which is to say,
get outta here, I'm not inviting you in.

If I want to purchase help of any sort
I'll go look for it on the internet
like any sane 21st Century Scholar
of the dawn of the era of the age
of the Post-plastic Afterlife.
Thank you, thank you, thank you,
get outta here, and good luck!

POETIC JUSTICE

Every spring someone knocks to tell me
they can replace my ancient front window, only
a nominal fee for glass and labor.
This year I knew the kid.
A former student, one of those Honors English boys
who cracked up at hotdog/dick double entendres,
raising one of their crew to sophomoric epic hero status
for writing an essay addressing options we all have
when wiping our asses. There below the front step
stood he, asking *can I cheat you*
on behalf of my fly-by-night employers
for the pittance of my slave's commission?
Haha! escaped my lungs. Haha! old anger swelling.
Ha, ha, haha, ha, I panted, delirious. I said, now look
at you. Look at what you've become. You stupid ass.

POEM WRITTEN AFTER SOME RANDOM GUY
WITH A CLIPBOARD AT MY DOOR ASKS
"DO YOU HAVE A SECURITY SYSTEM?"

I don't have much to steal. But
if I lost my records I'd probably die
of a broken heart. Certain things
are worth coveting. Clean air,
kisses, good beer. I wish I had
the ten best kisses I've been a part of
on a shelf in my living room.
I'd try them on to boost my spirits
and I'd rename my living room
my "that's really living!" room.
getting off is infinitely inferior
to kissing. There's the anticipation.
With kissing, things will only escalate.
I wish I had an escalator in a secret passageway
hidden in the basement I could mount
arriving at the top in your room.
That'd give us something to kiss about.

A CRAZY LITTLE THING

I have expressed my undying, infinite, deathless, permanent love
to every girlfriend, every fleshy love interest with a brain and various
squeezable parts, every receiving end of every liaison, more or less,
give or take, roughly speaking, since divorcing the wife I also expressed
my undying, infinite, deathless, permanent love for,
in a cute little ceremony by Pike Lake, where my mother cried,
but not for the reasons one might hope she would. I tell every woman
whom I long for, upon the development of the longing, that I could,
I may very well, I may already, love you forever. I am warning you,
ladies: I am apparently a batshit lunatic. I do not understand myself.
You should probably not date me, unless you feel prepped for
intermittent doses of crazy like shot glasses filled with
strange, idiosyncratic neurotransmitters producing odd euphorias
of affection and considerable herky-jerkiness of psychological selfhood.
Currently, though, if you must know, not that you asked,
although I will tell you anyway, I have a thing going on
with an adorable intelligent woman who again inspires me
to imagine myself in some sort of hero role in a Princess movie,
like Westley, pretty much, like I'm motherfucking Westley
in *A Princess Bride*. I call this thing "having a thing"
rather than "dating" because she says she "doesn't like labels"
which is no big deal, it's probably a lot better for me to think
of the thing as "not a Huge Big Thing" as I am not currently
possessed of any particular Thing that might be called Huge, Big,
although the lack of a label for the dating thing is curious, it's why
I'm calling this thing I'm reciting right now not a "poem"
but a "thing made of words" those words being "the shape
thoughts take" those thoughts being produced by
the language centers of the brain, that brain producing chemicals
to fire those thoughts, those words, this poem, that thing,
that thing I might be feeling for her, that indescribable ineffability
I'm too quick, too soon finding the words for, that effervescence,
that essence, produced upon certain kinds of human contact
by our lonely, melancholy, solitary minds.

REQUIEM

I wanna go back to the time of toaster ovens. To a Sears salesman
setting up an in-home demonstration of a behemoth microwave,
nuking a cake to cooked. I want my memories
not to have a half-life. Before sex offender lists.
Before computers running cars. When I walked home from 2nd grade
with an older boy who told me through my *ews* and *icks*
what his dad told him sex was, and assured me *but it feels good!*

I wanna travel down the telephone cord from the kitchen
to the living room where my mother sat in her chair
telling her mother a little too loudly how the kids were doing
in school. To the blue carpeted front room no one sat in til
I spent hours sprawled on the floor reading C.S. Lewis,
Tolkien, biography after biography. When mom and dad
would ask *are you sure you don't want to go out
and play with the neighbor kids?* I wanna go back

to the summer after 8th grade when he was home
from the hospital and whole in spirit and chauffeured
my first girlfriend and me to the movies telling bad jokes,
following *I got a million of 'em* with *they can't all be winners.*
Where we'd ignore *Arachnophobia* and lose ourselves
in each others' mouths. Back before the really bad things.

Before bitterness. Before I could take two right turns
on my bike out of the neighborhood to Oakwood
where he rested under a modest plaque marking his place,
already slipping, already fading, a memory receding
day by day in a tombstoned grassland, already not there.

A HIKE AROUND TOWN

All through this walk out of the neighborhood
past the Catholic church of my childhood
across the busy street, down the hill, under the train tracks
across another busy street
by the lake, and by the park, and into the woods
and out of the woods

I wanted to be alert to signals
I wanted my psyche-antennae perky and responsive
listening for visuals   watching for feels
for the sign we are constantly looking for
for the once living father   for the illusion of eternity
for the absent angels and their silent menace
for the orchestrator of the winds

for anything eternal to announce itself
people want this, I'm no different
we want a message, a sign
we want our cosmos Sentient and loving us
wanting us here   gifting us reason, meaning

but I walked home feeling slightly sick
and so temporary and so small

MATURATION

When I was in first grade at Sacred Heart Elementary
picking my nose and flicking it
in the manner of wishfully feral 6-year-olds everywhere,
the 6th grade class, the oldest, would gather
on our concrete playground lined with dodgeball circles
and spiked with the tether ball poles near which
Ricky Ramos flipped me crashing on the unforgiving
ash-black asphalt in second grade on my left knee –
and they would talk. That's all. Talk
and talk, grin around the circle with orthodontic beatifics
and discuss all kinds of things, maybe even
the kinds of things one wouldn't mention to a Priest.
I was not privy to these Indian-style-seating
roundpavement discussions with hands on knees,
I was busy reluctantly exchanging coats
with a frenemy who liked mine better than his
and whose social circle I so wanted to penetrate
I let him have his way with me. Why do they do that?
I asked my mom, an erstwhile public school teacher
who would join the Catholic staff
after I'd entered into the horrors of seventh grade.
"Oh, they're just *mature*. They're a *mature* group,"
she'd say, rolling that word around in her mouth
like it meant the Pope would soon canonize
our entire 6th grade class into sainthood.
That ended the discussion but not my curiosity,
but I could never get close enough to eavesdrop
successfully, nor could I allow myself to stand still
long enough to listen and to breathe. In the mystifying
fall of 1982 that dick who was wearing my coat
always had a dodgeball in hand
and was always taking aim at me.

MOTIVATIONAL

Everybody in South Bend knew Rudy
was an asshole. It was the truth.
The movie came out and he became
the world's worst motivational speaker.
Came here, once. I hear the speech
consisted of, look at me, I'm great,
can you believe it, maybe someday
they'll make a movie about you,
this is America, I'm great, all
the high class call girls know my name
when I visit Vegas . . . hang in there,
you too could win the American Fame
Lottery . . . This is an approximate quote
but gets at the gist of the message
fairly accurately. Educational Motivational
Speakers are peachy, they just love trying to convince
teachers that problems vanish via the panacea
of enthusiasm – also a general sense of love
and goodwill towards all people always,
which they have, and you, being the problem
person you are, don't. I heard one say
salesmanship is America's greatest contribution
to humanity and I wanted to barf on his shoes
purely for the principle of the matter
Our Principal was into it though, so
I kept my mouth shut. I just, you know,
I do it for the kids – like nobody else
does it for the kids – like nobody else,
nobody else does it for the kids like me.

OVER THE TOP

Once I had a young, pretty, smart girlfriend – supersmart!
A lot smarter than me at that age. I know, that sounds creepy
but it really wasn't. It was not a creepy relationship. I am not a creepy man.
Ahem. So once at my house we have all her young, hip, stylish friends over
to drink crap beer and White Russians or something ridiculous like that,
it was like theatre, they played the young and hip people, I played the older host
trying not to seem weird – have you ever tried not to seem weird?
You're guaranteed to seem weird trying not to seem weird – AHEM –
so we drank beer and listened to music from my generation
so I wouldn't feel so weird and we sat with our drinks
at the kitchen table and played euchre – Euchre! As if they were just a buncha
pre-middle-aged Hoosiers, like me! – and we're having a good ol' time
getting along and rocking to Modest Mouse and it's winter, people stepping
into the garage to smoke cigarettes, people using my toilet and thinking about
making out in a bedroom, and suddenly Spontaneous Arm Wrestling
breaks out – stealthy, like the Arm Wrestling was a team of Navy SEALs
that had just washed up on the shore of the kiddie pool frozen into the snow
in the backyard, it was kind of a freaky free-for-all really, it was kind of a
Love-In of arm wrestling, there was ambiguous sexual orientation arm wrestling,
mixed-gender arm wrestling, arm wrestling not ashamed to admit its mental health issues
and my ladyfriend goes CHALLENGE! or whatever and plunks her right elbow
on the table top and beckons me, I plunk my right elbow and grasp her hand
and we count ONE TWO THREE *whump!* Lickety-split, she beat me
just like that, and of course I've lost face, even though I'm fully aware
I have the arms of a spelling bee repeat champion, and I go "but I'm a leftie!
You know that!" as if I suspect she's conspired with her own reputation-assassinating
laser humiliation brainscope to humiliate me, and so *plunk! plunk!* Down go the left
elbows on the table, we count ONE TWO THREE and *nnnnnnnnnnnnnnnngggggg!*
nnnnnnnnnnnggggggggggggggggggggggg! nnnnnnnnggggggggggggggahhhhhhhhhh!
Whump! She elevates and celebrates in an adrenal rush of victory and she's dancing
around the room going Ooooga Oooooga! or whatever even though she's the least
cavewomanlike woman I've ever known, and I stand there ashamed, I stand there
ashamed til she turns and looks me in the face and oh, she says. A pause.
Goddammit, she says, because she's annoyed that I don't have the good manners
not to show humiliation in my face, a face like it was the day my grandpa died,
a face like it was the day my grandpa who'd lost an arm in WWII
to the teeth of a Nazi-trained wolverine died, my grandpa who'd raised me
from a feral 4-year-old human to a reasonable bourgeois adult with much browsweat
and concentrated intention, my grandpa who once drunk on Old Crow told me,
son, ya gotta love your arms son, ya gotta love and respect your arms, son,

you never know when one'll get bitten off by a Nazi-trained Stealth Wolverine,
ya never know, son, so love your arms, son, grow a third one, please?
Grow a third one and cut it off and sew it right onto my stump here,
A ha ha ha, a ha ha, I got a million of em! But seriously,
fruit of the fruit of my loins, fire of the breath of my flesh, ya know
you're gonna be a man someday, you are,
you're gonna know how to drive stick shift and you'll understand socket wrenches
and plumbing, ya gonna need your arms son, respect your arms, son,
and God in Heaven help you if you ever lost a dominant-hand arm wrestling match
to a beautiful gentle ruthless assassin brainiac young girlfriend.

RESOLUTIONS

I declare a New Year's in August
And for it I resolve
To be less of an asshole.
Not not to be an asshole
(we have to work with that
which is in the realm of possibility)
but more often than not, not an asshole,
and as such I pledge
to make a good faith effort
to avoid trolling political nincompoops on FB,
to treat all women as human people and not
as objects of my unbridled, misguided,
sad, hairy, suffering, idiosyncratic, bemused,
kerfluffled, kerplunked, middle-aged lust,
to suspend my belief in the inherent idiocy
of my obvious intellectual lessers
until such time as those lessers make their dumberness
so painfully obvious it needs not be pointed out,
to give guys in backwards baseball caps
a chance, I mean a real, honest chance,
to avoid calling out logical fallacies on FB
(as it turns out, people hate that)
to attempt to avoid calling the smarmy,
privileged, unearnedly-confident boyfriends
of my younger female friends "junior,"
to try not to yell at the kids
or the dog or the television or the oven
or the lawnmower and never to toss
my drumsticks across the basement
when I lose the beat, to thank my mother
continuously and with all my prodigal heart,
and to admit, bedgrudgingly, that
expensive though it was, that $9 halfpint
of Oskar Blues Quadrupel at Oak and Alley
was pretty damn delicious.

THE LOTTERY WINNER

A friend called to say something happened
and told a story with a long lack of buildup to a climax that
he won big money on two scratch-offs two days in a row

a grand, then another 500

Great fortune for him, this November of need
For a down payment for new wheels as the Miata
he was borrowing from parents finally took a total shit

But when such things happen, something in us
tells the Universe "This is not Enough"

And so what he was really calling to boast about
was the Powerball ticket he'd bought half an hour ago
at the same BP gas station where he'd gotten the scratch-offs

And to say that he was going to buy me and my family
a large house in which all four children would have rooms
of their own and God knows what else,

I'm gonna do that for ya, he said, I'm gonna get'cha a house,
I'll buy ya a house, my friend

And something in me recoiled at how good this made him feel
how he'd earned some sort of status, some canonization
or self-administered Medal of Honor

For this phantom largesse, this generosity of spirit but not wealth
which now only required the wealth to prove the spirit,

No fair, I wanted to say. Time out. Time. Let's have a do-over.
I thought much better of you last week, when I called asking you
to pick me up some cheap beer, and you did, my very good friend,
and when I said how much you said *don't worry about it,*
I'm sure you'd do the same for me.

GROWING UP IN THE RIGHT COMMUNITY

That's right, Cynthia
is dating John now. John Ableson.
Well, he comes from a good family.
We don't go to their church
but their church is not unlike ours.
He gets good grades. He's good
in Science but realizes
some theories are just theories.
He's a good athlete, a good teammate.
A strong leader. He can be dominant.
He works a good job in the summer.
A lot of running around. No,
not in that sense. A lot of running
around at his job, his summer job.
Lives on the lake, yes. Yes,
his parents own a nice home.
They drive nice cars. He's been over
for dinner a few times. I loved it
when he knew which fork to use.

HOW IT COULD'VE WENT DOWN IN THE FACULTY LOUNGE

Some of us sit on the left side of the lunch table.
Others occupy the far right. We're a microcosm
of America, that way (all the brains at our end,
of course). Down right way, the man at table's head
(how typical) says *they're making political nonsense*
of this religious freedom law. All it does
is give business owners a choice (to deny services
to gay people, we snarkily and parenthetically comment
from the side of truth and righteousness). Let's say
Mr. Christian Righteousness winged a tater tot our way, pegging our
(egalitarian, forward-thinking) department head
between the eyes while barking *Your Move,*
Sugarlumps! She might respond (reasonably
fuming) *we may as well display the No Gays Served Here*
signs and deny them a place at the lunch counter
like it's 1964 and then the dude at the wrong end
would go, *whoa whoa whoa, it's a lifestyle, not a race*
and then we (quick-witted, clever as sin) would call the law
A Race Alright, A Quick Sprint Right Up Dumbf--k Mountain
and over there they'd howl (somehow carefully avoiding
any allusion to Ginsberg) about perspectives, about the right
to equal time in the debate, about the things
that make this country great; one might *say It's clearly*
in the Bible (which they did) to which our (fearless, forthright) leader
might respond (as she did) *it says a lot of things*
in the Bible and then (as she didn't, but could have)
I know what I would call a refusal to bake a wedding cake
simply because of who loves who
— *not who loves who* our opposition would respond
who has sex with who. Big difference there. And we'd call that
a deeply held conviction, they might say,
and *yeah*, we'd say, *a conviction, a conviction seems about*
(obviously bigoted and dead nuts to the) *right.*

FRANNIE LAUNCHES MY MODELLING CAREER

My mom said "your forgotten middle child needs attention"
so I took her after school to Zoyo for frozen yogurt
and good conversation. I told her when very little
I had night terrors about bees chasing me around
my bedroom and the bees were in formation behind me
They had faces, frowns, and big exaggerated downward-slanted
evil eyebrows, Frannie laughed and laughed, she thought
that was a riot, she said once she had a dream that she
was being chased by a Tongue Monster, it was made of
tongues, it looked like it had sharp teeth but as it came close
she realized those're tongues too, she woke to our dog Emma
licking her face. It doesn't matter to me if she
made that last part up because it makes for a better story
and I'm proud she's smart enough to know that.
For a time I sat and stared in the general direction
of the pavement with an ankle on my knee and my raised knee
cradled in my hands, Frannie said something about my
pondering pose, what a pondering pose, you ponder
like a rock star, dad, she said, I said yeah, I could be
a Ponder Model, so I tried it out, and whaddyaknow
I've got a skill, this is a new thing I can do,
soon I will be pondering life the universe
and the yogurt uncomfortably inhabiting my stomach
on a page or screen near you, someday I will be
The World's Greatest Ponder Model, I didn't really
mean to, I wanted to be a writer, but I want to leave
my kids a legacy, I want to show them one can aspire
to something greater, and if your goal in life
or even some random thing you came up with
on the spot that doesn't mean anything is to model
pondering for the most exclusive ad agencies in the country,
then you can do it, you sure as hell can, don't
give up, try your best, never quit trying.

WELCOME TO DADLAND!

Kids'll drive ya nuts
on a snow day. I teach,
so I'm home with them.
I yell at excessive volume
to be quiet and then I yell
excessively for slamming doors.
Welcome to Dadland!
Hypocrisy Reigns!
I just hope nothing happening
today with redlining emotions
will permanently fuck them up.
But who knows, you know?
Who knows what they will say
to their friends as they grow old,
and older. Who knows
the stories they will tell.

SINGLE DAD BLUES

Eight days without kids at 39
is sizing up to be less than
the weeklong party you were dreading.
Friday, Saturday, you got drunk each night
with a different close friend who calls you best,
on Friday you hug one woman who tells you your poems
are amazing and on Saturday you ask another out
but she declines by Sunday and it didn't mean
much to you anyway. Now it's Monday evening
and you've worked and walked the dog and
walked yourself from one near outdoor bar
to the next, where it's alright with you
to be drinking only iced tea. 90 humid degrees,
you've got no appetite and no one nearby
to check up on. No one tonight will be asking
for shelter from their bashful nightmares
in your too-big bed. Within 3 years
the dog will die, one more than that
and your oldest will reside elsewhere, maybe
forever. What would you tell her mother about her
now, if she were here to listen as if she understood?

GRATIFICATION

It seems I can't quit
drinking, stay off social media,
and start exercising seriously
all at once, so I'm going
for 2 out of 3. The drinking stays.
Talk about a no-brainer. Facebook
makes me feel bad. Exercise
makes me feel good. Drinking too,
of course. I'm reminded of the '90s
when we were all into the idealized '60s
and I owned 2 Jimi Hendrix T-shirts,
one black, one tie-dyed purple.
"It was a *selfish* time," our English teacher
told us. "The prevailing idea was
'if it feels good, do it'." I'm surprised
I still remember this, as I spent
most of high school daydreaming
about the moment I could close
my bedroom door each afternoon
and all-naturally inseminate a wad of Kleenex.
They say delayed gratification
makes a more successful man, and I'm proud
to report I never saw the need
to ask for the restroom pass 10 minutes before
the bell to call in some left-handed relief.
Perhaps that's why so many things I have foreseen –
the stacks of notebooks, the beer gut, the poetry
fixation – have come to fruition.

NEW INSCRIPTION AT ELLIS ISLAND

Welcome to America, friend! Our country's poor
are generally unintelligent and obviously morally repugnant.
You should hate them! Hate them with all your heart!
Hate them like Jesus would! The poor people
in your country are noble and trustworthy,
bravely suffering, uncomplaining – they should
be lionized, then martyred and/or given Bibles
with their free meals because it would be morally repugnant
and/or stupid to feed a starving person without informing him
of the Good News – the best news! The lovely news,
God stood by and watched while we murdered his Son.
He said, Ok! Murder my Son! Murder my Son,
that'll fix things! That's how God told us he loves us,
see? God loves us because he let us murder his Son.
God also loves entrepreneurs and people who shit
in their own drinking water. God loves fracking.
Frack it up, God says! Frack away, I'll trade you
some earthquakes for some fracking. Wheeeee!
Wasn't that a fun ride! Let's do it 00 times a year
from now on! I love you, I love you all, I love you
so much, God says. I even love your unborn children
until they become selfish, entitled, stupid American
poor people, and then I'm like, meh. I'm like,
let's not educate them – one needs One Book Only
for a good education anyway. And I'm like,
let's not feed them. That is not the correct answer
to What Would Jesus Do. And then I'm like,
let's spend shit-tons of money coming up with new ways
to murder mass populations of people. Let's build
so much murdering equipment we have more murdering
equipment than the next 20 countries, and we could murder
and murder, we could murder for weeks, we could murder
til we eradicated the very idea of murder because nobody'd
be left to murder – so we'll murder the populations of poor
and useless people in our country, and then we'll murder
the middle class, especially the ones who oppose our murdering.
We'll murder them first. And once all our enemies and envyists
are gone I guess we'll just murder each other, and finally,
finally – finally, America! Our problems will be solved.
Enjoy your stay.

THEORIES

Afterbirth is gross; it's also
everything that happens to you in life.
The afterlife? Everybody's got a theory,
some say souls are recycled, newly incorporated
in perpetuity, some say it's nothing,
like the taste of water or calling clear a color.
Vonnegut called it a violet light and a hum,
at least that was Billy Pilgrim's experience.
A Harvard neurosurgeon reported
in his recent near-death experience
angelic beings, breathtaking, gasping-in-awe-inducing,
producing overwhelmingly pretty noises,
perhaps Gregorian chant or the harps of cliché,
perhaps a sound like a semi trailer made of diamonds
and pure unadulterated love whooshing by
on a celestial highway. On a highway,
not everybody is stoned, and on a freeway,
prostitutes only work on a volunteer basis.
I feel like I could work in a "pro bono" joke here.
The surest way to evade both opportunity
and unpleasantry is to volunteer
for nothing, always. I'd volunteer
for a near-death experience, but
I am frail in spirit and faint of heart,
and I fear I'd fear what I found,
or what I didn't, or, even worse, I'd be mistaken.

PRESS RELEASE, MOON EDITION

On behalf of the moon, the moon
had nothing to do with it. Your crazy students.
The E.R. on Halloween. There was no moon
on Halloween. On Halloween, the moon
did not exist. On behalf of the moon,
blame it on somebody else this time.
The moon neither confirms nor denies
any role in the batshit neighbor hopping
leg to leg on the lawn brandishing
an ancient flintlock. Some things,
the moon says, shaking it's head.
Some things I just can't take credit for.

DEAR INTERNET,

Do you have any idea
how I can relieve nagging back pain
with a simple, soothing yoga pose?
Many a year through trouble and strife
I have been searching, seeking and googling
for a simple, soothing yoga pose.
My dog died. My wife left me. My car
broke down. My winky stopped working
and yet I assured myself, if only I could find
a simple, soothing yoga pose.
We make life so complicated sometimes.
Why can't we all love each other,
make love, be love, hate hate, rejuvenate
with a simple, soothing yoga pose?

BACKYARD HAIKU

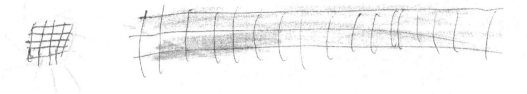

summer wind: a miracle only made
more lovely by a backyard beer, a notebook

                                        I can almost see
                                        my childhood bedroom from here

        all my children learned
        to ride a bike lickety-split
        like, oh duh

                                    air kicking on
                                    birds quieting themselves
                                    before a storm

imagine how badass
birds would be with arms

I grew up in this neighborhood
the trees still watch over us
like sentinels

cemetery's not far
wherever my father is
it isn't at his grave

so much depends upon
the grill in my backyard
dinner, for instance

SITTING IN A PLASTIC LAWN CHAIR IN MY OWN BACKYARD, INDIANA, MAY 2015

A neighbor's mower just quit,
bird sounds echo in the trees.
The shriek of car and motorcyle
to the distant right. Here, the maple tree. There,
the soccer net, the neighbor's still trampoline.
I've got a novel, a book of poems,
a notebook, and a lager.
The kids are fed and settled.
The dishes stay undone.
I am not wasting my life.

FINALE

Everybody dies
at The End,
doofus.
That's the finale
of every story
ever told.
No exceptions.
No variations.
No resurrections.
No reincarnations.
Poof.
Fin.
Gone.
All of us
hurtling toward
planets fumbling
through the universe.
Even you,
kid. Even you,
my friend.

NOTES ON THE POEMS

Ode to Facebook – The quote from Orwell occurs at the moment Winston learns to love Big Brother. "Hear me now and believe me later" is the catchphrase from Dana Carvey and Kevin Nealon's "Hans and Franz" Saturday Night Live sketch from the 1980s.

I'm Pleased My Boy Dances – "Mr. Henn esq./ "if you're nasty" is a reference to "Call me Janet. Miss Jackson if you're nasty" in the Janet Jackson song "Nasty Boys."

Prosperity Gospel – For a real life example of one of these charlatan preachers see Joel Osteen.

Today in 7th Period – "Johnnie Sue" is a generalized stand-in character name coined by Coach Al Rhodes at Tiger Basketball Camp, Warsaw, IN, in the 1980s.

This One Time – This challenge really happened, but in reality I spelled "diarrhea" wrong. Missed that 2nd "r."

Over the Top – The poem title is a reference to an '80s Sylvester Stallone movie about a trucker who enters a national arm wrestling tournament.

How It Could've Went Down in the Faculty Lounge – A dramatic re-enactment of a much more boring, mundane moment of department lunch time tension.

Gratification – "Our English teacher" is the legendary Jack Musgrave, the greatest English teacher to ever grace the halls of Warsaw Community High School.

NOTES ON THE ART

What follows is a commentary on each of the illustrations in the book. Oren and Lucy were quite forthcoming in discussing the ideas behind their work and will do most of their own talking. Frannie was willing to share, although at times the explanation was complicated enough that I needed to paraphrase it. Zaya, the oldest and most advanced artist among my children and inventor of the cover image for this book, was less willing to provide commentary, preferring to let her work speak for itself, so in places I have substituted some of my own impressions of her contributions. - SH

Cover – Zaya: "This is a concept for a weirdly-structured being, devoid of emotion." What Dad sees in the cover image is a strange clown with a front butt who may have pee'd his pants. Dad finds this hilarious. And an entirely fitting image for the "Noble Sad Man" sensibility that the poetry attempts to project.

Dedication – Lucy: "That was just a random picture I drew. It's mainly about how they're teasing him because of his long nose, and they're dipping his head in the toilet."

Acknowledgments – Lucy: "He's a fancy elephant man; he just got his brand-new fancy striped pants. He's watering his garden by blowing water out of his nose so that the water goes onto his roses and his strawberries and his tomatoes. He's also growing pumpkins."

Contents – Zaya: "It's a cloud with a horn. I don't think there's much more substance to it than what it is." Here Zaya begins to resist explaining her own artwork. Which is something she has in common with many noteworthy poets.

After Epigraph – Oren "That's the sunshine men. The fancy one [on the left] is the older brother, the one in the middle is the dad, and the other one is the younger brother. The dad is like the rock star one, the rock one, the punk rock one." Oren takes care to note the Mohawk on the middle figure.

13 Oren: "That's a mutant shark." Why does he have so many fins and eyes? "I don't know. It's a mutant?"

19 Zaya: "I don't know. I drew that a year ago. You can say he's battling his inner demons if you want to make a made-for-TV movie of it." And this is where the sixteen year old, with her snark, her anxiety, and her touchy wit, was excused from commenting any further on her work.

21 Oren says this is a hot dog world of hot dog men fishing for hot dog fish. The hot dog fish are going to be eaten by the hot dog shark, but the hot dog shark is going to get hooked.

23 Oren. Dad neglected to ask him about this one. Really, Oren does too much talking anyway (if you'd like to hear more Oren talk look him up on twitter at @PearlsofOrenism), so we'll let this one go.

24 Oren: "It's a bacon man wearing a suit and tie. He's red and white and he's not a crispy bacon or a fat bacon. He's a WEIRD bacon."

27 – Lucy (at the bottom): "He's Frankenstein, but she doesn't have any arms. Frankenstein tried to grow a new arm for her, but it came out of her head. They're married. And they live in this big creepy house that everyone thinks is haunted but they're nice."
Lucy (at the top): "This is a bowling pin guy who goes bowling." There's a lot more to that story, but it's too complicated for Dad to take down successfully.

29 Lucy: "Mustache bird is a fancy bird, and he just got a fancy haircut, and he's going on a date to Hacienda with his fiancée, Senorita Beardo. Cuz she has a beard. She's a bearded bird."

30 Oren: "My friend told me to make a zombie guy, I forget what his name is [the zombie guy, not the friend – Dad], and he described him, and that's what I came up with." He drew this one as part of a series of morning journal drawings in first grade, at school. And God bless Oren's schoolteachers for encouraging him.

35 Lucy: "He tried to do a bunch of experiments on himself, but it all went wrong, so that's why he has eyeballs." She notes he also tried to turn his hand into a laser gun, and also that "he's freaking out."

38 Frannie: "That was from sixth grade. I think I was really tired. I drew the teeth first and then decided, that's the dude I wanna draw."

45 Zaya: A giant slice of pizza foregrounded by an apparently sad clown. Why is the clown sad? Is it because he prefers vegetarian pizza but this one has pepperonis? We'll never know. The artist refuses to interpret her work.

47 Lucy: "That's a punk rock unicorn" [Lucy was a punk rock unicorn for Halloween this year, 2016]. "And that's a cheeseburger guy who loves cheeseburgers. He's a cannibal because he eats them. That's why his girlfriend is a hot dog."

48 Frannie reports that this was a complicated work of free-association that started with an inadvertent hole in the elephant.

51 Lucy: "That's a crazy mad scientist and his name is Alberto. He used to be bald, but then he did an experiment on himself to give him hair, but now he can't comb his hair down; it has a mind of its own. Its name is Orange. And it talks."

54 Frannie: She says, "That's just a clock dude," and fails to elaborate with the creativity of a Lucy or an Oren.

61 Lucy: "That's an evil monster that isn't actually evil. He's nice to his minion. And that's why the minion is so nice to the monster. If you have a minion, and you're mean to it, it will run away."

64 Zaya: This is an image of some sort of chaos. Dad's not quite sure what it's all about, but he thinks it complements the poem admirably.

67 Zaya: Various doodles, mostly faces. Zaya is an incessant doodler. Dad thinks she decided to get into art because she started doodling and couldn't stop.

70 and 71 Oren: "That's flannel world. You know the flannel shirts I have? So like, everything is flannel like that." Why? "I'm pretty sure that day was picture day and I was wearing my flannel shirt and my khaki pants."

72 and 73 Frannie: On the original, most of the flowers are black and white, and the one in the middle is supposed to look like a sunbeam, and is rainbow-colored with an emphasis on reds and oranges and yellows. Frannie interprets "live colorfully" thusly: "Well, the other flowers were more bland, and the one in the middle stands out more, and holds its ground."

74 Lucy: "His name is Pedro, and he's very nice. And he always gives everybody grapes because fairies don't live near grapes, but they love grapes. And he saved the Magical Cow King." Dad would like to note that it provides a clever and fitting counterpoint to the sadness of the final poem.

Back Cover – Zaya: "It's just a cool dude in boots." Dad is interested in the posture. Does he (she? they? it?) have to go to the bathroom? It sure seems like it. It sure seems like whatever it is, they're having an emergency.

GRATITUDE

I would like to thank the following people for their roles in creating this book and their continued support for my anxious, mixed up life:

Joe Chaney, my immediate editor at Wolfson Press, for helping shape this book into something it could not have been without him.

Sky Santiago, designer of this book, Sky selected the images and fit them with the poems expertly, and I'm grateful. Also, Tera Cuskaden, editor, for getting the project started.

Ken Smith, Wolfson editor, and the Wolfson editorial board, for agreeing to take on the manuscript.

Oren, Anna, Kaveh, Dave T., Sarah and Erica, Clayton, Cracker and Natty, Clint, Grochalski and Malinenko for their solidaritous sensibilities, my inner circle of poet-people excluding one (stay tuned, below).

Lydia, may she rest in peace, for saving my life by giving me 4 beautiful children.

My mom, my sister and brothers, encouraging supporters of my attempts at poetry whether they understood or agreed or not.

James and Jay: twenty more years and we may be living together as Golden Boys.

Kosciusko County Kettleheads Brewclub – Cheers. Christmas Party Poems Until I Die.

Dave G and Oak and Alley public house and Three Crowns Coffee, for the generous use of their facilities for poetry shows.

American Legion Post 49, Warsaw, IN, for the open mic hosted by Josh, then Amanda, then Marena . . . I think Brett was the man in there for a short period, too. And Mike and Josie and Bruce. Stalwarts.

My colleagues in the local high school English department. Good teachers worth more than what they're being paid, who do more than what they're paid for.

But most especially Don Winter, who I took a fiction class and a poetry class with when I was an English major at IUSB, and who is an excellent poet with relevant working class poetic theories, and who told me, at a time when I wasn't sure if it was true or not, that I was good enough.

Steve Henn is the author of *And God Said: Let there be Evolution!* (NYQBooks 2012) and *Unacknowledged Legislations* (NYQBooks 2011). He's a full time dad, a full time high school English teacher, a frequent reader of O.P.P. (other people's poetry), and an occasional drummer in ersatz basement bands. He's been a featured reader at the Uptown Poetry Slam, the Indianapolis Poetry Slam, and in the IUSB Fall Writers Series. Indiana's insane state legislature has yet to drive him out of K-12 education, but they're getting close.

The cover and interior were designed by Sky Santiago.
The poems are set in Avenir Book.
Book title, author name, acknowledgments,
poem titles, and page numbers
are set in Lemon Yellow Sun,
a hand-printed typeface created by David Kerkhoff
at the Hanoded Type Foundry.

YOUR DOODLES HERE

YOUR DOODLES HERE

YOUR DOODLES HERE

YOUR DOODLES HERE

YOUR DOODLES HERE

YOUR DOODLES HERE

Made in the USA
Charleston, SC
09 February 2017